Math in Focus®

Singapore Math
by Marshall Cavendish

Student Book
Kindergarten Ⓑ
Part 2

Author
Dr. Pamela Sharpe

U.S. Consultants
Andy Clark and Patsy F. Kanter

 **Marshall Cavendish** Education

US Distributor

 HOUGHTON MIFFLIN HARCOURT

COMMON CORE

© 2012 Marshall Cavendish International (Singapore) Private Limited

Published by Marshall Cavendish Education
An imprint of Marshall Cavendish International (Singapore) Private Limited
Times Centre, 1 New Industrial Road, Singapore 536196
Customer Service Hotline: (65) 6411 0820
E-mail: tmesales@sg.marshallcavendish.com
Website: www.marshallcavendish.com/education

Distributed by
Houghton Mifflin Harcourt
222 Berkeley Street
Boston, MA 02116
Tel: 617-351-5000
Website: www.hmheducation.com/mathinfocus

Second edition 2012

Math in Focus® Kindergarten B Part 2
ISBN 978-0-547-62535-5

Printed in Singapore

6 7 8   1401   16 15 14 13
4500403739   B C D E

Contents

Lesson 1 Comparing Lengths

Draw a long tail.

Draw a short tail.

Draw a longer object.

 1

2

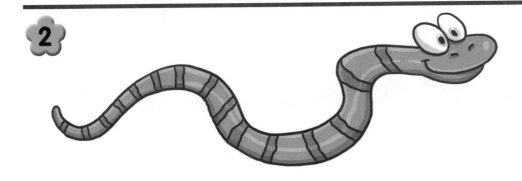

Draw a shorter object.

 1

 2

Make an X on the kite with the longest tail.
Circle the kite with the shortest tail.

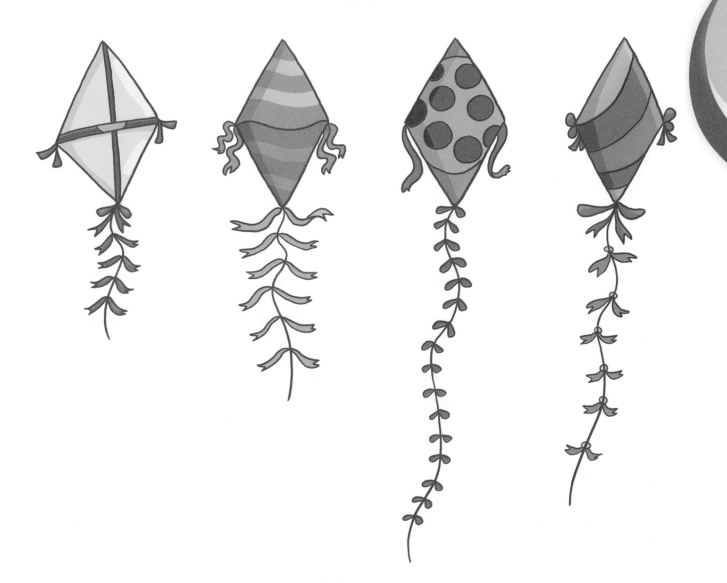

Lesson 2 Comparing Lengths Using Nonstandard Units

Measure, count, and write.

The pencil is about _____ cubes long.

The spoon is about _____ cubes long.

The toothbrush is about _____ cubes long.

The comb is about _____ cubes long.

The tube is about _____ cubes long.

The paint brush is about _____ cubes long.

Count and write.

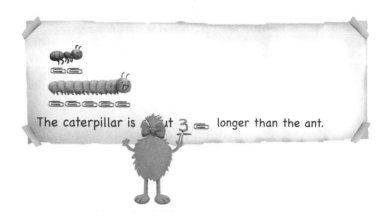

The caterpillar is about 3 📎 longer than the ant.

1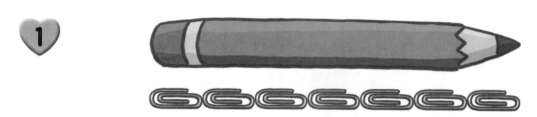

The pencil is about _____ 📎 long.

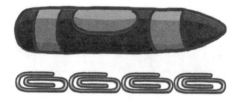

The crayon is about _____ 📎 long.

The pencil is about _____ 📎 longer than the crayon.

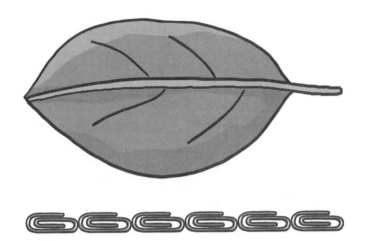

The leaf is about _____ 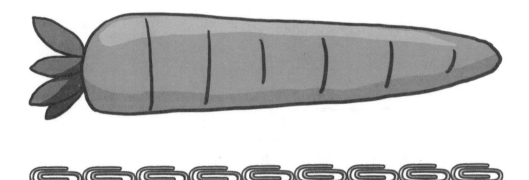 long.

The carrot is about _____ long.

The leaf is about _____ shorter than the carrot.

Comparing Heights Using Nonstandard Units

Count and write. Make an X on the taller vase.

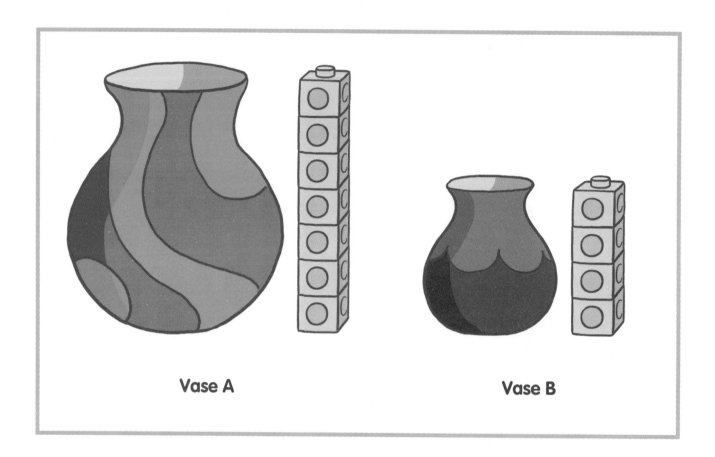

Vase A   Vase B

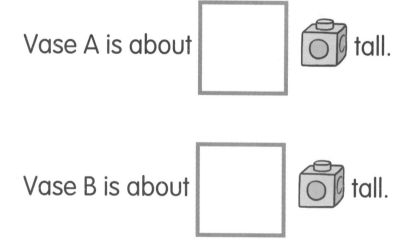

Vase A is about ☐ tall.

Vase B is about ☐ tall.

Count and write. Circle the shorter flower.

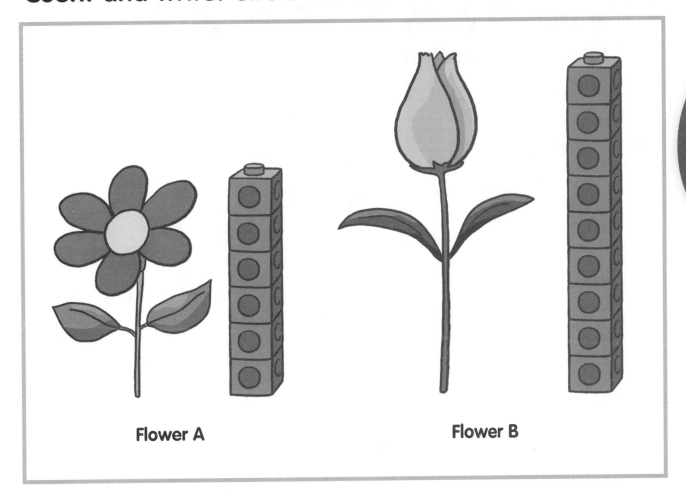

Flower A

Flower B

Flower A is about ☐ 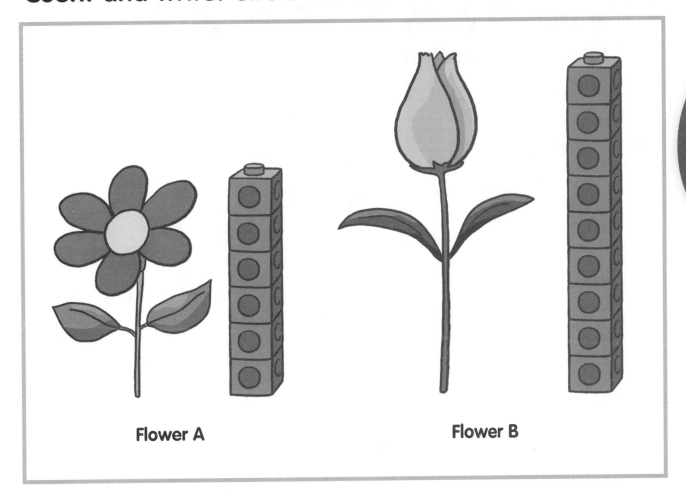 tall.

Flower B is about ☐ tall.

Lesson 1 Classifying Things by One Attribute

Sort and match.

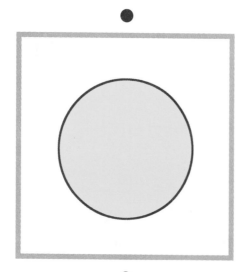 

2

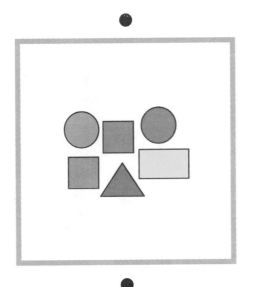

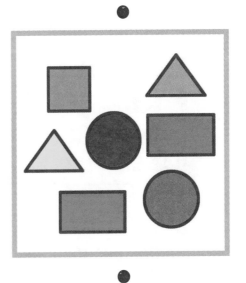

Sort and match.

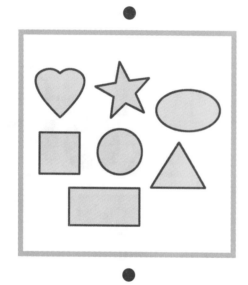 

4

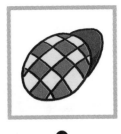 •

 •

 •

•

•

•

•

•

•

•

Make an X on the item that does not belong.

   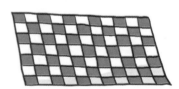

Match.

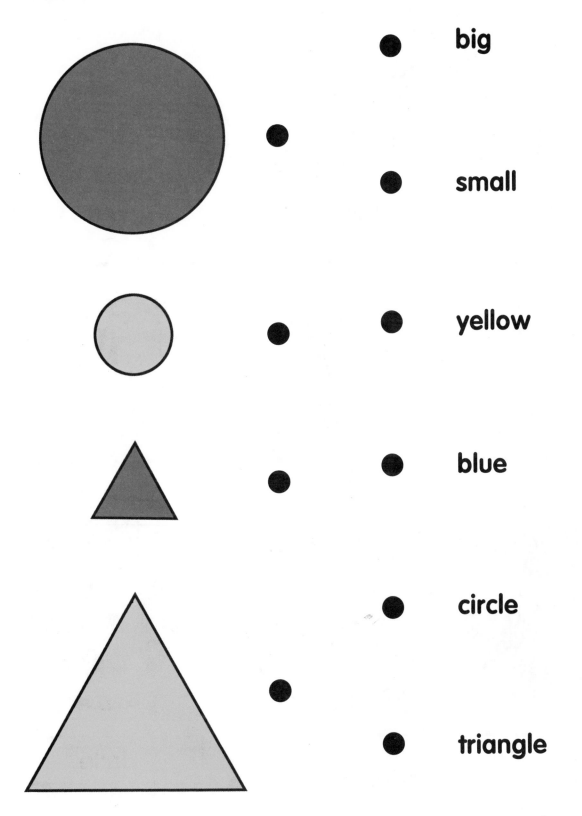

• big

• small

• yellow

• blue

• circle

• triangle

Make an X on the wrong common attribute.

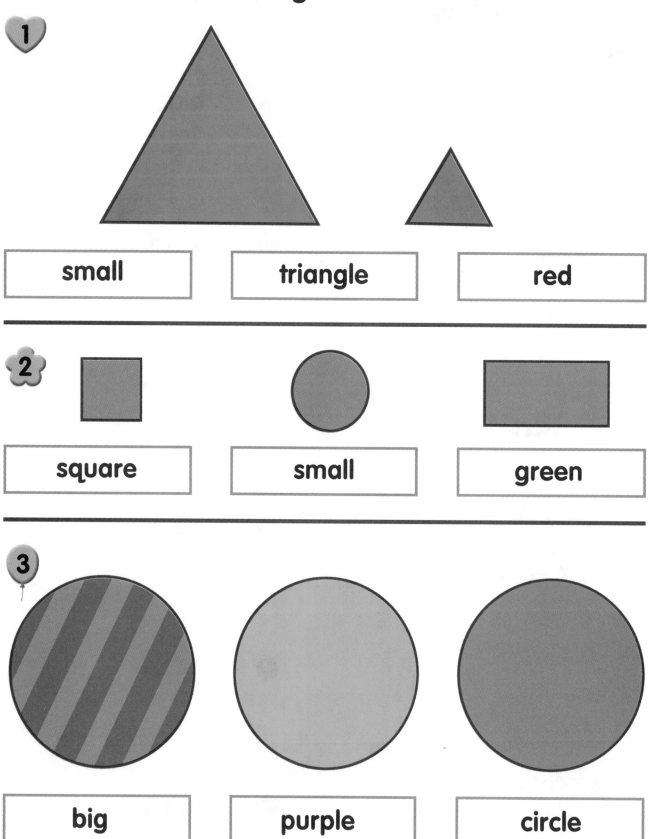

1

| small | triangle | red |

2

| square | small | green |

3

| big | purple | circle |

17 Addition Stories

Lesson 1 Writing Addition Sentences and Representing Addition Stories

Count and write.

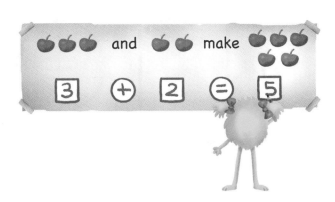

🍎🍎🍎 and 🍎🍎 make 🍎🍎🍎🍎🍎

3 ⊕ 2 ⊜ 5

1

 and  make

4 + 3 = ☐

2

 and  make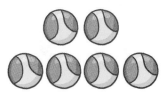

2 + ☐ = ☐

Count and write.

 3  and  make

☐	⊕	☐	⊜	☐

 4

  and  make

☐	◯	☐	◯	☐

5

 and  make

☐	◯	☐	◯	☐

Count and write.

Count and write.

 2

 3

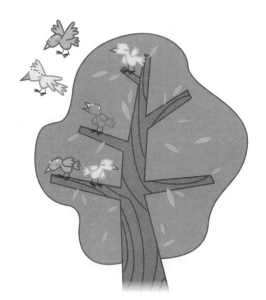

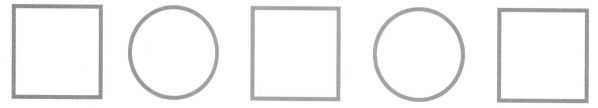

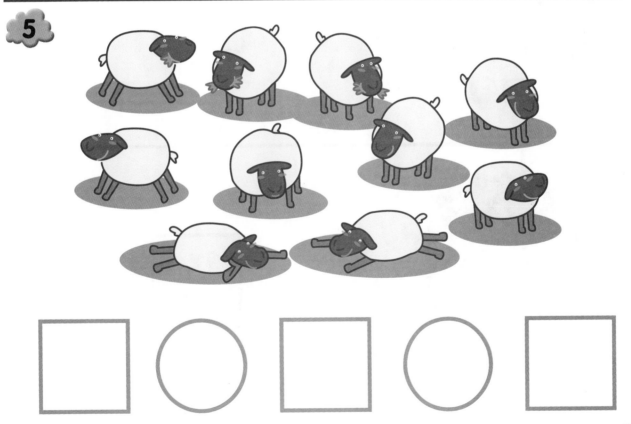

Lesson 2 Addition Facts to 5

Fill in the missing numbers.

1 0 and ☐ make 5.

2 1 and ☐ make 5.

3 2 and ☐ make 5.

4 3 and ☐ make 5.

5 4 and ☐ make 5.

6 5 and ☐ make 5.

Lesson 1 Writing Subtraction Sentences and Representing Subtraction Stories

Count and write.

There are 4 ducks.

2 ducks walk away.

How many are left?

4 ⊝ 2 ⊜ 2

There are 5 bananas.

2 bananas are eaten.

How many are left?

 ⊝  ⊜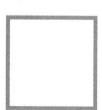

5 ⊖ 2 =

2

There are
7 candles.

Take away
3 candles.

How many
are left?

3

There are
9 pencils.

Take away
4 pencils.

How many
are left?

    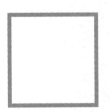

Count and write.

    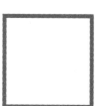

Count and write.

How many more? Circle. Write the number sentence.

1

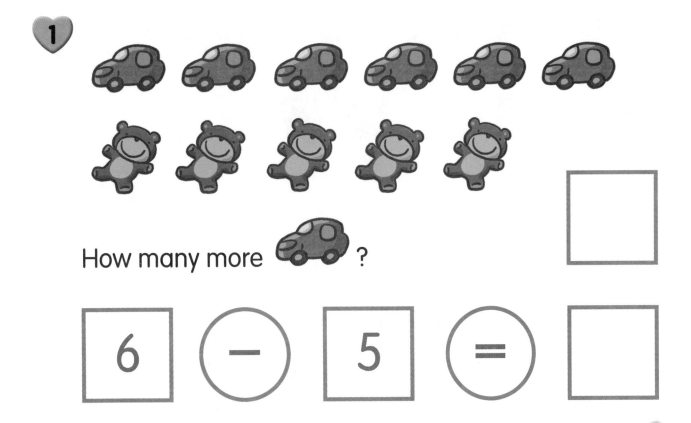

How many more? Circle. Write the number sentence.

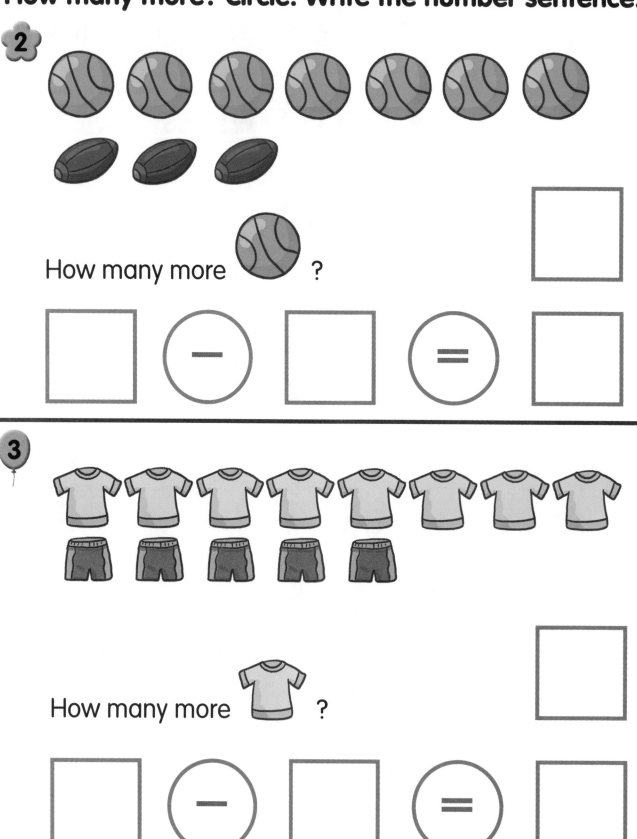

2

How many more 🏀 ?

☐ ⊖ ☐ ⊜ ☐

3

How many more 👕 ?

☐ ⊖ ☐ ⊜ ☐

4

How many more ?

5

How many more  ?

How many more? Write the number sentence.

1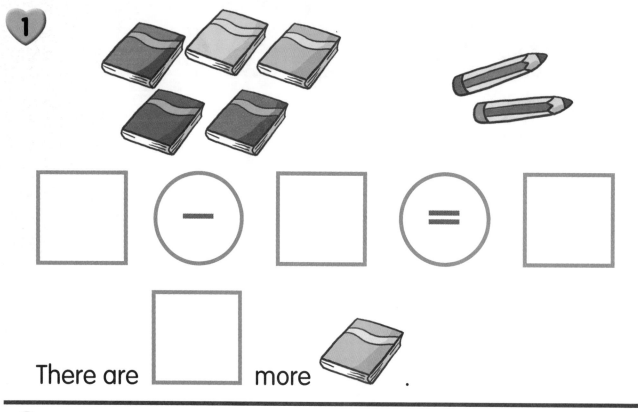

$\boxed{}$ $\bigcirc\!\!-$ $\boxed{}$ $\bigcirc\!\!=$ $\boxed{}$

There are $\boxed{}$ more .

2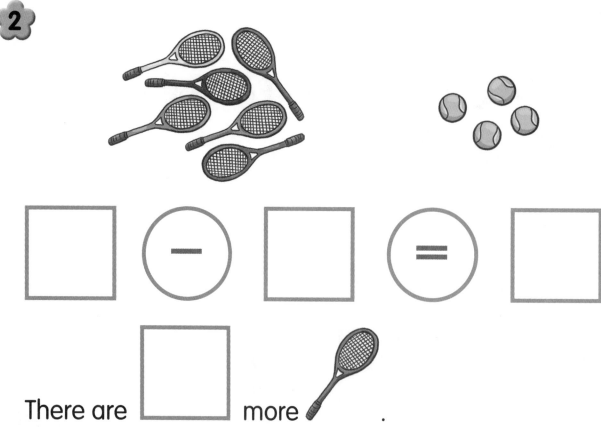

$\boxed{}$ $\bigcirc\!\!-$ $\boxed{}$ $\bigcirc\!\!=$ $\boxed{}$

There are $\boxed{}$ more .

3

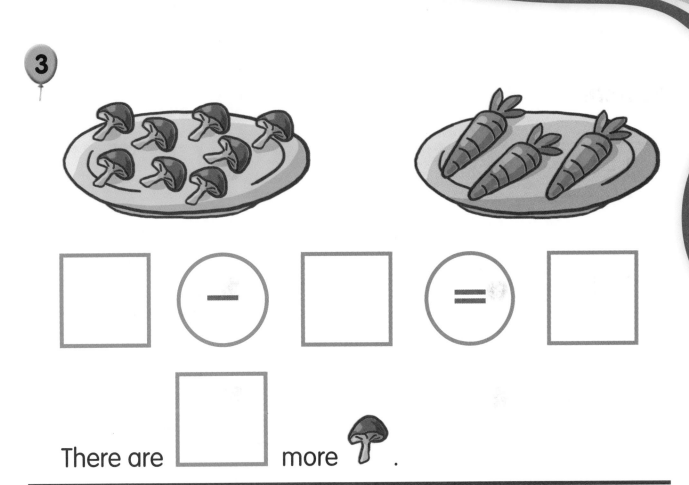

$\boxed{}$ $\bigcirc\!\!-$ $\boxed{}$ $\bigcirc\!\!=$ $\boxed{}$

There are $\boxed{}$ more 🍄 .

4

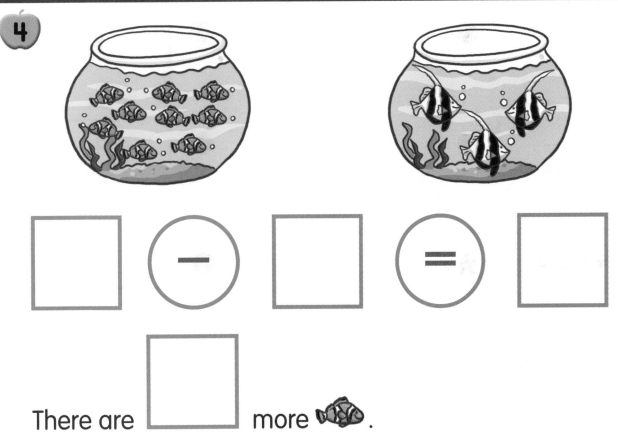

$\boxed{}$ $\bigcirc\!\!-$ $\boxed{}$ $\bigcirc\!\!=$ $\boxed{}$

There are $\boxed{}$ more 🐠 .

Match.

$3 - 1 =$ ●		● 0
$2 - 1 =$ ●		● 1
$4 - 3 =$ ●		● 2
$5 - 0 =$ ●		● 3
$1 - 1 =$ ●		● 4
$4 - 0 =$ ●		● 5

Complete the number sentence.

1 5 - 4 = _____

2 3 - 3 = _____

3 4 - 2 = _____

4 1 - 0 = _____

19 Measurement

Lesson 1 Comparing Weights Using Nonstandard Units

Circle the heavier thing.

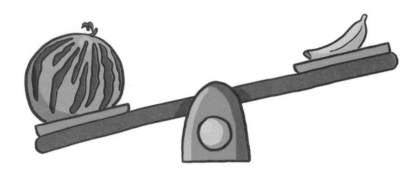

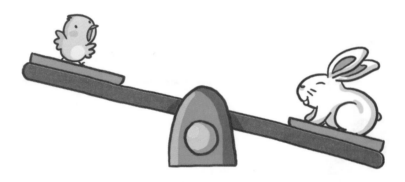

Circle the lighter thing.

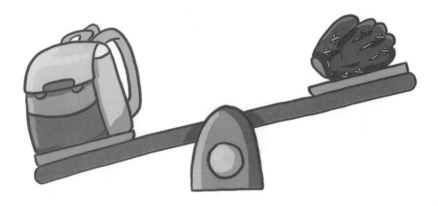

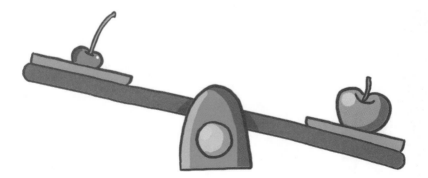

Count and write.

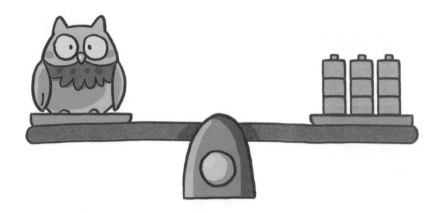

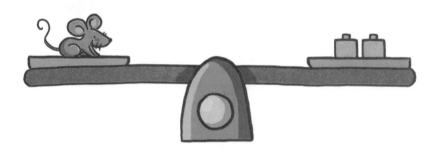

The owl weighs 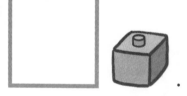.

The mouse weighs 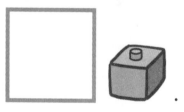.

Circle the heavier animal.

Count and write.

The teddy bear weighs  .

The doll weighs  .

Circle the lighter thing.

Lesson 2 Comparing Capacities

Circle the container that holds more.

 1

2

 3

Circle the container that holds less.

Color the containers that hold the same amount.

1

2

3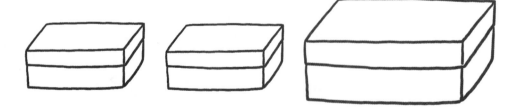

Lesson 3 Comparing Events in Time

Which takes more time? Circle.

1

2

Which takes less time? Circle.

1

2

Lesson 1 **Coin Values**

Match.

 •   • 5¢

 •   • 25¢

  •   • 1¢

 •   • 10¢

How many pennies do you need? Color.

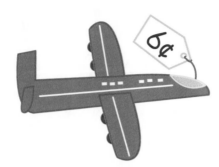

 and

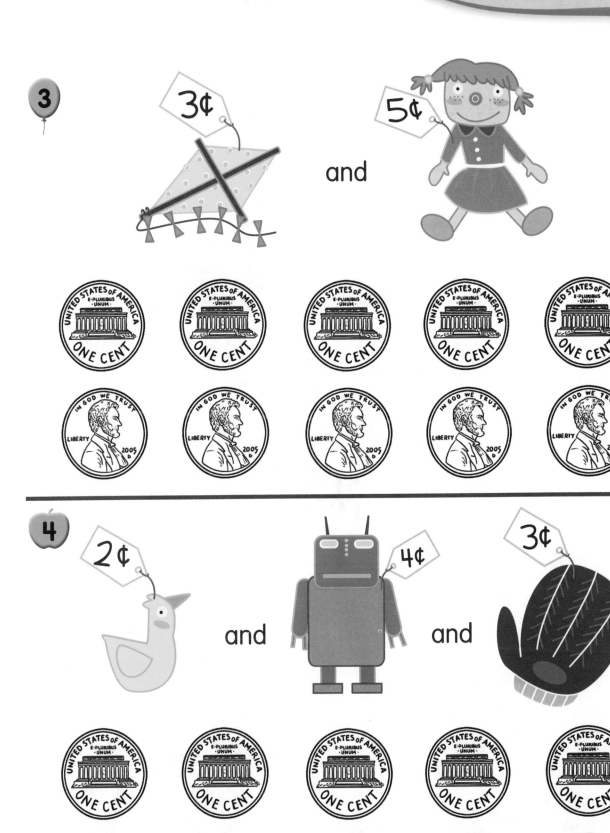

3 3¢ and 5¢

4 2¢ and 4¢ and 3¢

How much is needed? Circle the purse.

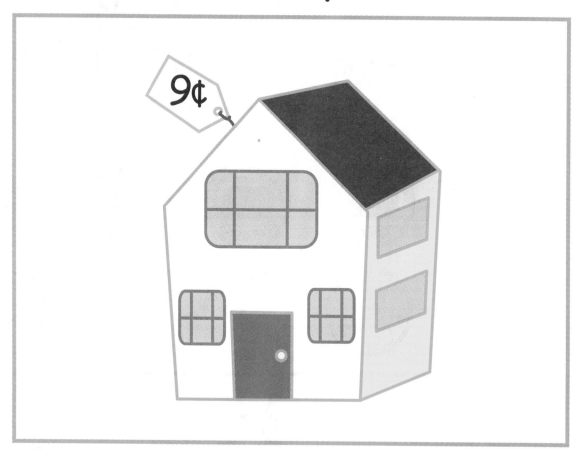

9¢

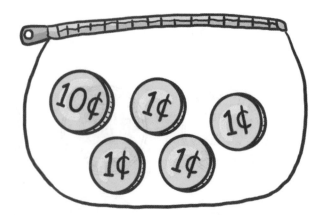

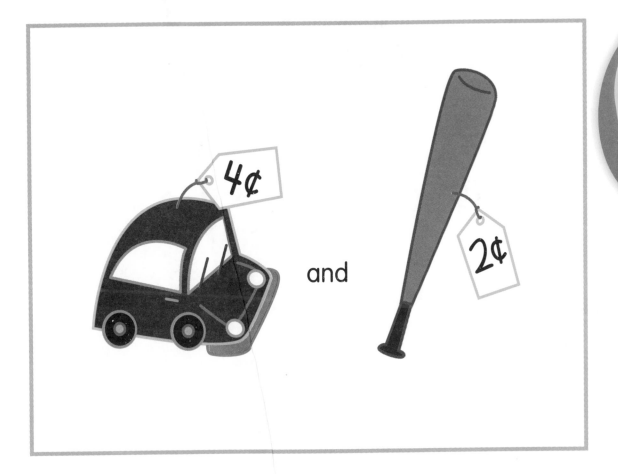

and

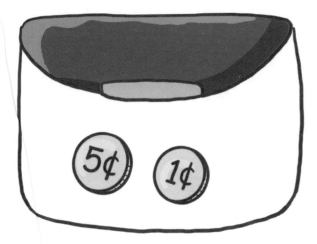